GOD'S SPECIAL PROMISES TO ME

CHARLES MILLS

GOD'S SPECIAL PROMISES TO ME

A devotional book for young children

CHARLES MILLS

Pacific Press Publishing Association
Boise, Idaho
Oshawa, Ontario, Canada

Edited by Jerry D. Thomas
Designed by Dennis Ferree
Cover photo by Charles Mills
Inside photos by Charles Mills
Typeset in 11/13 Janson Text

Unless otherwise stated, all Scripture verses in this book are
from the International Children's Bible.

Library of Congress Cataloging-in-Publication Data:
Mills, Charles, 1950-
    God's special promises to me : a devotional book for
early readers / Charles Mills.
        p.   cm.
    ISBN 0-8163-1147-1
    1. Children—Prayer-books and devotions—English. 2.
God—Promises—Juvenile literature. I. Title.
BV4571.2.M54   1993
242'.62—dc20   93-17945
                                                    CIP

                                                    AC

93 94 95 96 97 • 5 4 3 2 1

Dedication

To my wife Dorinda
And the little girl who lives
in her heart.

I love you both.

Preface

Hello, boys and girls. This book is just for you. Read the words carefully. Look at the pictures thoughtfully. I want you to discover how much Jesus loves you. Maybe, as you enjoy this book, you'll get some new ideas about how you can love Jesus in return.

Also, I want you to learn how to love others. We're all children of God. Someday we're going to live together in heaven. Let's start being happy together right here on earth, OK?

Remember, God thinks you're wonderful. And so do I.

Your friend,
Charles Mills

God Never Leaves Me

ast week my grandfather died. He got really sick and then went to the hospital for an operation. He didn't make it. The doctor said his heart wasn't strong enough.

Grandpa used to take me for walks on the beach by his house. We'd watch the waves roll across the sands and talk. He'd tell me a funny story, and I'd laugh. Now I can't laugh anymore.

Just before he got sick, Grandpa taught me a Bible verse. He made me memorize it so I

could repeat it without looking at the words. This is the verse: *"God has said, 'I will never leave you; I will never forget you'"* *(Hebrews 13:5)*.

Now, when I walk along the beach, I know God is still with me, even though Grandpa has gone away.

Maybe that's why he taught me the verse. He knew I'd be sad, but he didn't want me to feel lonely. Grandpa wanted me to know that God will never leave me.

God Will Teach Me

o you know what wisdom is? I didn't know, so I asked my dad. He's smart.

Dad said wisdom means that you understand something. When my dog barks at the door, I let him out. When it's cloudy, I take my umbrella to school. I'm using wisdom when I do these things.

But there's a lot of stuff I don't know. Like why my friend Daryl got sick, and how birds can fly so high.

Dad read me a verse in the Bible that says, *"If any of you needs wisdom, you should ask God for it. God is generous. He enjoys giving to all people, so God will give you wisdom"* (*James 1:5*). He may use a parent or teacher to help Him, but what matters most is that God makes sure I learn what I need to know.

It makes me happy to know God loves me so much that He wants to be my teacher.

God Helps Me Be Strong

 have a little brother. His name is Andrew. Sometimes he can get on my nerves.

He likes to sneak up behind me and scare me. I jump. He laughs. Very funny.

I love Andrew. Really I do. It's just that he makes life rather difficult sometimes.

But God wants me to keep on loving my brother no matter what he does to me. Here's a verse I like to read whenever Andrew acts silly. *"The person who continues to be strong until the end will be saved" (Matthew 24:13).*

This means that if I have patience and don't lose my temper, Jesus will help me love Andrew every day. I want to go to heaven with Jesus. I want Andrew to go to heaven too. So I don't fuss at him or tell my mom or anything. I just sit there and try my best to be strong. Loving someone isn't always easy, but in the long run, it's worth it.

ne day my mom and I were out mowing the lawn. Actually, she was mowing, and I was helping to pick up the grass clippings.

All at once, she stopped the mower and ran a few steps ahead. She reached down and picked up something.

"What's the matter?" I asked, walking to her side. Then I looked in her hands. "Oh," I gasped. "It's a little bunny."

Mother nodded. "I saw it in the grass and didn't want it to get hurt." She gently stroked the soft fur. "That's why I did what God does."

"What God does?" I repeated.

I'm Safe

Mother smiled. "There's a verse in the Bible that says, *'Hold thou me up, and I shall be safe' (Psalm 119:117, KJV)*. When danger comes, God says He will hold us close and keep us safe."

I looked at the little animal and touched its tiny nose. "Thank You, Jesus, for keeping me and this bunny safe today," I said.

God Forgives Me

ast week I made a big mistake. My mother asked me if I had finished all my vegetables. I said Yes, but that was a lie. I had given my vegetables to our dog Archibald. He'll eat anything.

After I told the lie, I felt sick inside. I tried to play with my trucks, but I started feeling worse and worse.

Finally, I remembered a verse my Vacation Bible School teacher had read. It says, *"If we confess our sins, he will forgive our sins. . . . He will make us clean from all the wrongs we have done"* (1 John 1:9).

Then I knew what I had to do. I knelt right there beside my toy truck and asked Jesus to forgive me. Next, I ran to find my mother and told her that I had fed my vegetables to Archibald.

Mother smiled and hugged me. Suddenly, I didn't feel sick anymore. I felt great! I went back to playing with my trucks, happy to know that when I do something wrong, God will forgive me and make me feel good again.

I Give
to God

 have a job. Well, it's not a big job. You see, I help my neighbor, Mrs. Martin. Every day I stop by her house and make sure her little pet bird has plenty of food and water. Then I clean out his cage and try to teach him how to talk. So far, all he says is *tweet, tweet*.

She pays me ten dollars a month. I told her I'd do it for free, but she said she wanted to pay me because I do such a good job and never forget.

When I get my money, I do what my dad does. I sit down at the dining-room table and carefully print my name on a tithe envelope. Then I place one dollar in the envelope and seal it up. When I go to church, I drop my tithe into the offering plate with a big smile on my face.

Why do I smile? Listen to this verse from the Bible. "God loves the person who gives happily" (2 Corinthians 9:7). I smile because I'm glad God gives me the opportunity to help Mrs. Martin. I smile because I like working. And I smile because God lets me keep all the rest of the money for myself.

Jesus Will Come Again

 ne of my favorite stories in the Bible is about when Jesus took His disciples to a mountaintop. He told them how much He loved them, and then He began to rise up in the air.

The disciples were surprised. When Jesus disappeared from view, they were very sad.

All at once, an angel appeared and said, "Why are you so sad? Jesus will come again."

This made the disciples feel a lot better. Would you like to know what it will look

ike when Jesus comes again? Listen to this
Bible verse. *"Look, Jesus is coming with the clouds.
Everyone will see him" (Revelation 1:7).*

Someday, Jesus will come through the clouds.
Isn't that exciting? Now, when I look up into
the sky and see a bunch of clouds drifting by, I
feel happy inside. Someday I'll see Jesus up
there. And best of all, He'll see me and invite
me and my family to go home with Him to
heaven. Hurry, Jesus, and come again! I'm waiting for You.

God Listens When I Pray

ach night, before I go to sleep, I kneel beside my bed and talk to God.

I tell Him Thank You for giving me food to eat and a warm house to live in. I ask Him to help my friend Sarah, who is sick, and my big brother Chris, who goes to high school. He says some of his friends want to do stuff he doesn't want to do. That's why I always remember Chris when I pray.

Does God hear me? Of course. He promised He would. Listen to this Bible verse I learned. *"I will help them while they are still asking for help" (Isaiah 65:24).*

That means while I'm talking to God, He's busy answering my prayer. He's sitting beside Sarah's bed, watching over her. He's walking with my brother Chris as he goes to the mall with his friends, ready to help him say No to bad things they want him to do.

I sleep all night, knowing that God listens when I pray.

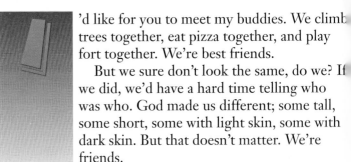

'd like for you to meet my buddies. We climb trees together, eat pizza together, and play fort together. We're best friends.

But we sure don't look the same, do we? If we did, we'd have a hard time telling who was who. God made us different; some tall, some short, some with light skin, some with dark skin. But that doesn't matter. We're friends.

Someday we're all going to live in heaven with Jesus. How do I know that? Because

24

God Wants to Save Every-one

there's a verse in the Bible that says, *"Anyone who believes and is baptized will be saved"* *(Mark 16:16)*.

I'm glad it says *anyone*. It doesn't matter if you're short or tall or whether you have light skin or dark skin.

All of my buddies agree that when we get to heaven, we're going to keep right on playing together. You can come join us because God wants to save everyone. That means you too.

God Helps Me Escape From Satan

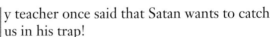

y teacher once said that Satan wants to catch us in his trap!

"What kind of trap is it?" I asked. "Does it have big, steel bars all around it?"

"No," my teacher said. "It's not the kind of trap you can see or touch. It's a trap that makes us do bad things like lie to our parents, argue with our friends, or hit someone with a stick."

"Oh," I said. "It's like a sin trap."

"Exactly." My teacher nodded. "Satan wants to make us do things we know are wrong. When we're bad, he's caught us in his sin trap."

Then she smiled. "But God wants to help us. Listen to this verse in the Bible. *'Praise the Lord. . . . We have escaped like a bird from the hunter's trap' (Psalm 124:6, 7)."*

"I understand," I said. "When Satan catches us, God helps us to escape." I'm glad God does that, aren't you?

ast Sunday, my mom took me to the zoo. I love going there and seeing all the animals.

My favorite is the hippopotamus. Now, there's a funny-looking animal! It has a great big mouth and little, tiny ears. It has a huge, round body and short, stubby legs. Even its tail is funny.

As we were standing there watching the hippopotamus, my mother said, "Isn't that animal beautiful?"

"What?" I gasped. "He's funny looking! And he just sits around all day. He doesn't do anything important."

"God doesn't think so," she continued.

God Made Everything Good

"There's a verse in the Bible that says, *'God made the wild animals. . . . [He] saw that this was good' (Genesis 1:25)*. If the Creator made all the wild creatures, we shouldn't think they're ugly or not important. We should love and take care of them, no matter what they look like or do."

We watched the hippopotamus yawn a big yawn. "If God says he's good," I announced, "then I think so too."

Jesus Is My Shepherd

 ometimes when we go for a ride in the country, we drive by a farm where there are lots of sheep. We stop at the fence and watch the wooly animals eat grass under the trees.

Then the shepherd comes over and talks to us. He's the man who takes care of the sheep. He tells us how he feeds them, protects them, and makes sure they have plenty of water to drink.

To the shepherd, sheep are very important. He spends every day watching out for them.

My dad says Jesus takes care of us like a shepherd takes care of his sheep. Listen to this verse he taught me. *"The Lord is my shepherd. I have everything I need" (Psalm 23:1).* As long as I want Jesus to be my shepherd, I will have food to eat, water to drink, and a safe place to live.

Thank You, Jesus, for being my shepherd.

Jesus Wants Me to Go to All the World

'm a missionary! So are my friends.

Would you like to know why we're missionaries? Because we want Jesus to come soon. Listen to this Bible text. *"The Good News about God's kingdom will be preached in all the world, to every nation. Then [Jesus] will come"* (Matthew 24:14). So you see, we've got to stay busy telling others about Jesus and His love so He can return.

If you want to be a missionary too, here's what you do. First, ask Jesus to help you be kind and forgiving. Next, listen carefully to the stories in church. Ask your mom or dad to teach you some Bible texts so you can repeat them without any help.

Then, when someone looks sad, just say to them, "I'm sorry you're sad. Would you like me to tell you a Bible story?"

That's what a missionary does. If everyone did that, Jesus would come tomorrow!

God Has Great Love for Me

ne day, my dad came home from work very tired. He went straight to the couch and lay down.

I felt a little angry. My dad works hard, so when he comes home, he doesn't have any energy left to play catch with me.

Then I heard him call my name. "Jonathan? Would you please bring me a glass of orange juice? I'm thirsty."

At first, I didn't want to do it because he didn't play catch with me. Then I remembered a Bible verse my dad had read just a few days before at family worship. It said, *"Lord, you are kind and forgiving. You have great love for those who call to you" (Psalm 86:5).*

I felt ashamed. If Jesus has great love for us when we call to Him, shouldn't we have love for our moms and dads when they call to us?

I hurried and got my dad a big glass of orange juice. If that's what Jesus would do for me, then that's what I'm going to do for others.

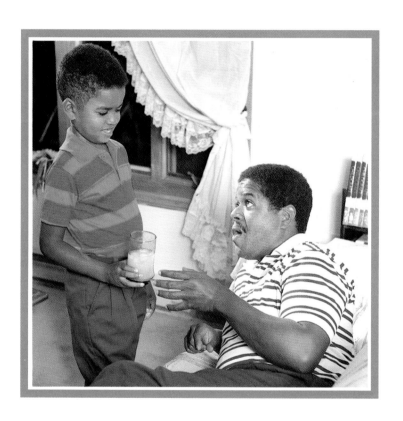

very morning, out on our back porch, a squirrel comes to visit. He sits on the railing and waits for us to bring him some nuts.

Mom makes sure he gets plenty.

"Remember that Bible verse we read yesterday morning?" she asked. "It says, 'God fills the hungry with good things' (Luke 1:53). So when I see the little squirrel begging for food, I know God wants me to fill its tummy with fresh, tasty nuts."

I frowned. "How about when *people* are

God Knows When I'm Hungry

hungry? Does God want us to help Him fill their tummies with good things too?"

"Oh, yes," Mother said. "That's why we take bags of groceries to the community soup kitchen every month. We're trying to make sure all the tummies in our town get filled with good things to eat."

I watched the squirrel munch on his nuts. "God fills the hungry with good things," I repeated. I was glad I could help.

Jesus Asks Me to Give to the Poor

 oday I saw something that made me feel sad. While my mom and I were in town, I noticed a man pushing a shopping cart. There were no groceries in the cart, only some dirty, old boxes; a couple of bottles; and a torn, faded coat.

"Who is that man?" I asked my mom. "Where does he live?"

Mom shook her head slowly. "He's a street person and doesn't have a home or any food. Everything he owns is in that shopping cart."

Then Mom looked at me. "Do you remember the Bible verse we read a few days ago that says, '*Give to the poor, and you will have treasure*

in heaven' (Matthew 19:21, NIV)?" I nodded.

"Let's do what the verse says," Mom called out. We drove right home and collected some tasty vegetables from the garden. Then we went back to town and found the man with the shopping cart. "These are for you, sir," Mom told him.

The man smiled. "Thank you," he said. That night, when Mom and I ate supper, the vegetables tasted extra good.

Jesus Gives Me Rest

 y bedtime, I'm usually very, very tired. I've studied my lessons, played with my best friend Anthony, helped Dad take out the garbage, walked the dog, washed my face, brushed my teeth, and let Mom chase me up the stairs.

When I snuggle under the covers, I fall asleep fast because my body is tired.

There's a Bible text I think about every once in a while. It says, *"Come to me, all of you who are tired and have heavy loads. I will give*

40

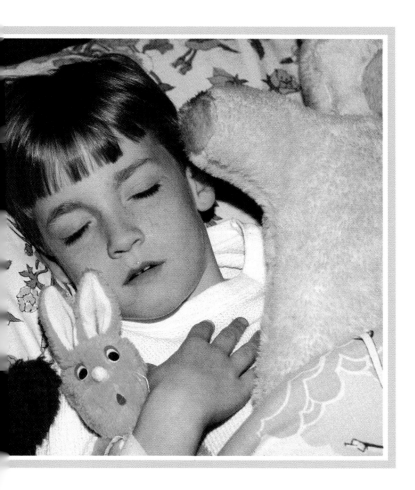

you rest" *(Matthew 11:28)*.

Jesus understands that sometimes our *minds* can get tired too. Like when we're worried about stuff or are feeling afraid. He wants to give our minds rest. So He invites us to pray and ask Him to help us know what to do.

Then our minds *and* our bodies can rest all night long.

I Search for God

 love family worship. Each evening, after the supper dishes are washed and dried, my little brother and sister, Mom, Dad, and I sit down on the couch. We read a Bible story, sing a song, and pray. It's lots of fun.

We started having this special worship each day when Dad read a verse from the Bible that says, *"When you search for me with all your heart, you will find me!"* *(Jeremiah 29:13)*. Whom are we searching for? Jesus.

No, we're not playing hide-and-seek with Him. We're searching for verses that tell us about His love, about how much He cares for us.

When we find a verse, we write it down on a piece of paper. Then, the next time one of us is feeling a little sad, we read the paper and remember that God loves us very much. It makes us feel happy again.

Searching for Jesus means learning how much He loves us.

Jesus Looks for Me

ave you ever been lost? I have. We were camping in the forest, and I went for a walk. Suddenly I didn't know where the camp was. I didn't know where anything was! It was scary! Was I ever glad to see my parents again.

There's a verse in the Bible that says, *"The Son of Man came to find lost people and save them" (Luke 19:10)*. My dad told me this means Jesus wants to help people who are doing things they shouldn't do. He said sinning was like being lost. It makes you feel afraid and lonely.

Now, when I tell my friends the story of when I was lost in the forest, I also tell them

about how Jesus looks for lost people and
wants to save them. When you're lost, you're
afraid. But when you're found, you're one
happy camper.

 like to read about wild animals. Maybe I'll build a zoo someday, I don't know. But whatever I do, I'm going to keep learning about bears, tigers, lions, rhinoceroses, antelope, and all the other neat creatures God made.

The more I read about these animals, the more amazed I get. I've seen pictures of mountain goats walking along high, narrow cliffs. How do they do that? One book shows dolphins jumping above the water. How can they swim so deep in the ocean when they have to breathe air just as we do?

Last week my teacher read a verse in the Bible that says, *"God can do everything!" (Luke*

God Can Do Everything

1:37). I nodded and said, "That's for sure." Then I started thinking. If God can do everything, He can help me with every problem and every worry I have.

Now, when I look at my animal books, I know that if God can make all those wonderful creatures, *nothing* is too hard for Him to do.

God Knows When I'm Lonely

ometimes I feel all alone, like when I get home after school and my mom and dad are still at work or when no one chooses me for baseball.

I just want to cry.

When I feel like that, I repeat a verse I learned at Vacation Bible School. It says, *"You will cry out to the Lord, and he will say, 'Here I am'"* (Isaiah 58:9).

Then, I close my eyes and pray, "Please, Jesus, help me feel happy again." After that, I get busy cleaning my room, or I go push one of my classmates on the swings. Pretty soon, I've forgotten how lonely I felt. I'm too busy having a good time.

I don't like being lonely. But Jesus hears me when I pray and says, "Here I am. I love you. I'll help you be happy again." And He does!

God Knows My Name

This is my puppy Snowball. I call him that because when he was very little, he looked like a snowball rolling across the grass.

My puppy likes to play with me. He barks and jumps up and down whenever I come around. He even knows his name.

When I say, "Come here, Snowball," he runs right to me and licks my face.

When I say, "Sit, Snowball," he wags his tail and barks. He hasn't learned that trick very well yet.

Did you know that God knows your name? There's a verse that says, *"I have called you by name, and you are mine"* (Isaiah 43:1).

Imagine, the God of the whole universe knows each of our names, just as I know Snowball's name. That's neat.

When I'm feeling a little sad, I remember that God loves me so much, He even knows my name. Then I feel better and go play with Snowball. I gotta teach that dog how to sit!

he other day my mom read a verse in the Bible that made me excited. Here's what it said. *"If you believe, you will get anything you ask for in prayer" (Matthew 21:22).*

Wow! Anything! I told my mom I was going to ask for a new skateboard, the one with the monkey painted on it.

Mom shook her head. "That's not what the verse means," she said. I was a little confused.

"Jesus promises to give us any *spiritual* thing we ask for," she continued. "He'll help us build our faith in Him. He'll teach us how to be more loving and forgiving. Jesus will even show us how to be more obedient to our

Jesus Answers My Prayers

teachers and parents if we ask Him to."

I thought and thought. Yes, I could use some help in those areas. So, now, when I pray, I ask Jesus for spiritual things, not just toys and stuff. And I know He'll answer my prayer. He promised!

I Am Not Ashamed

ast week at church, my teacher, Mrs. Albertson, asked me to read a text from the Bible. I didn't want to, because I'm shy.

"Come on, Sidney," she said with a smile. "You read so nicely. It's just one small verse."

"OK," I finally said, but I wasn't too happy. I was afraid the other kids would laugh at me.

I took the Bible from my teacher's hands, and she showed me which verse she wanted me to read. I cleared my throat and began. *"I am not ashamed of the gospel, because it is the power of God for the salvation of everyone who believes" (Romans 1:16, NIV).*

What was this? Jesus doesn't want us to feel embarrassed or shy when we read the Bible or tell others about His love? The teacher nodded with a smile. "You did just fine," she said.

As I sat down, I hoped Mrs. Albertson would ask me to read again real soon. Next time, I won't be ashamed.

God Wants Me to Be Peculiar

'm peculiar. Do you know what that means? Peculiar means I'm different. I do stuff my own special way. Let me explain.

When some of my friends are cheating in school or saying bad things about their parents, I'm studying my lessons and saying good things about mine.

When neighborhood kids are fighting and calling each other names, I'm trying to play fair and not get mad when someone else wins the game.

When other kids don't go to church, I ask my mom or dad to take me each week so I can hear exciting stories and sing new songs.

Why am I peculiar? Listen to this text I learned. *"If ye will obey my voice . . . then ye shall be a peculiar treasure unto me above all people" (Exodus 19:5, KJV)*. I want to be a treasure for God, so I'll keep on doing things a little differently. Want to join me?

God Teaches Me How to Love

e have a new baby sister named Yondela. My big brother and I are very proud of her. We hold her gently and feed her her bottle when she cries.

Before she was born, I asked my mother to teach me how to love and take care of a new baby. Mother opened our worship Bible. "Listen to what Jesus said," she told me. "*'You must love each other as I have loved you' (John 13:34)*."

Mother closed the Bible. "So you see, if you want to love and take care of someone else, think about how Jesus loves you; then do the same."

I thought and thought. Jesus always listens when I talk to Him. He helps me when I'm sad. He protects me from danger. And He makes sure I have food to eat and a safe place to sleep.

"I'm going to love our new baby just like Jesus loves me," I said. And that's exactly what I do.

God Heals Me

L ast week I had a bad cold. I sniffled and sneezed all day long. My mom sent me off to bed and made me stay there.

"Am I ever going to get well?" I sighed.

"Of course," she told me. "Jesus promised you would."

"He did?" I gasped.

Mom lifted my Bible from the night stand and opened it. "Listen to this," she said. "'*I will bring back your health. And I will heal your injuries,' says the Lord (Jeremiah 30:17).*" Mom smiled. "God wants us all to be healthy and happy."

"When will God heal me?" I asked.

"Sometimes it happens quickly," Mom said. "Or it might take many days or even weeks. And there are some serious sicknesses that will be healed only when Jesus comes again. But God will heal everyone."

I nodded, closed my eyes, and began waiting for Jesus to heal me. Now, I feel fine!

God Will Guide Me

have a little cousin named Megan. She's just one year old.

Sometimes, my aunt lets me play with Megan out in the front yard. We have lots of fun. I show her the flowers growing by the walkway, and we watch the birds flying in the trees above our heads.

If I weren't there to take care of her, Megan might wander away and get lost. But I make sure she's safe, and when we walk around, I hold her hand.

This makes me think of a Bible verse I learned in church. Listen, I'll repeat it for you. *"The Lord says, '. . . I will guide you and watch over you'" (Psalm 32:8).*

That's exactly what I'm doing for my little cousin. I'm guiding her and watching over her, just like Jesus does for me. He'll do that for you too. Aren't you glad He loves us so much?

Someday I'll Fly Away

oday was an awful day! I fell down and hurt my thumb, I spilled the milk at breakfast, my teacher gave me a "D" on my reading test, I struck out during the last inning of our baseball game, and my sister punched me in the ear. Today was the absolute pits.

My grandmother put her arm around me. "Let me read you a couple of texts from the Bible," she said. "Maybe they'll make you feel better."

She sat down beside me and thumbed through the pages. "Listen to these words spoken by David. *'I wish I had wings like a dove. Then I would fly away and rest. . . . But I will call to God for help. And the Lord will save me'* (Psalm 55:6, 16).

"See," Grandma said, "even David had bad days. He just wanted to fly away from his troubles. Instead, he asked God for help."

That evening, I went out to the field to fly my kite. It crashed, of course. But I knew no matter what my day was like, I could always pray to God, and He'd love me anyway.

God Makes My Daddy Happy

 love my daddy. He's strong, handsome, kind, and gentle, and he teaches me neat stuff, like how to climb a tree.

My daddy thinks I'm wonderful. He says so!

I like to make him happy. As a matter of fact, God helps me do that. Listen to this verse the preacher read in church last week. *"The father of a good child is very happy"* (Proverbs 23:24).

Kids can make their parents happy just by being good. You don't have to get all "A's" in school. You don't have to be beautiful. You don't have to know how to play baseball. You just have to be good!

That means we should be kind and loving, sharing our toys with our friends and doing as we're told.

My daddy smiles when he sees me doing nice things for others. I smile too. Making my daddy happy is my favorite way of showing him how much I love him.

God Rules the Sea

ave you ever visited the ocean? My family went to California once. We drove along the Pacific Ocean all day. It was beautiful!

Sometimes we stopped and walked down to the shore. It was a little scary. Those big waves came rolling in and crashed against the rocks. *Swush! Splash!*

"Don't be afraid," Dad said.

"But the waves are so big," I cried.

Dad nodded with a smile. "You need to learn a new verse," he said. "Listen. *'You rule*

*he mighty sea. You calm the stormy waves'
Psalm 89:9).*"

I looked out across the shore at the roar-
ng waves. With a loud voice, I shouted,
You rule the mighty sea. You calm the
tormy waves." Then I smiled. Even though
he ocean still scared me a little, I knew that
vhen waves are crashing on the rocks, God
nows what's going on and can hear me
vhen I call.

God Wants to Save All People

This afternoon I was walking along the beach with my Uncle Mike. He's not really my uncle, but I live with him, and he takes good care of me.

We stopped and sat down to watch the waves wash up on the shore. "Hey, check this out," he said, pointing down by his feet. "Look at all the colorful stones. Each one is different, but they're all part of this beautiful beach. Sort of reminds me of something."

"What?" I wanted to know.

"Well," Uncle Mike continued, "I read a verse in the Bible that says, *'God wants all people to be saved' (1 Timothy 2:4)*. It doesn't say just white people or black people or people with tan or yellow skin. It says *all* people.

"This beach is beautiful because of the many colors and shapes of the stones. That's how heaven will be—filled with people of all colors and races. Won't that be great?"

I nodded. If heaven is like this beach, it will be a wonderful place to live.

t first, they're afraid. But I stand really still and hold out my hand. They'll come when they discover that I have bread crumbs.

Slowly they begin to edge closer. I call softly. They swoop down and look at my hand. They see what I have in it. Soon they learn to trust me and enjoy the food I've brought.

When I feed the sea gulls at the beach, I remember a Bible text I learned in church

God Will Give Me a Kingdom

school. It says, *"Don't fear, little flock. Your Father wants to give you the kingdom" (Luke 12:32).* It makes me think of Jesus holding out His hand to me, telling me how much He loves me and my family.

But He doesn't have bread crumbs in His hand. Oh, no. He has scars there from the nails the soldiers used to fasten Him to the cross. He's trying to give us love and a wonderful new home in heaven.

My Name's in the Book

collect baseball cards. It's fun to gather all the players from a team and place them together in their own box.

On the back of the cards I find information about the baseball player: how many hits he's had, his home runs, his times at bat, where he was born, and what teams he's played for. When I read the card, I know a lot about that player.

I learned a verse in the Bible that tells me God has a book in heaven that's sort of like my baseball-card collection. Guess whose name is in that book? Mine! Yours too. Isn't that neat?

God knows all about me. He knows what I

like and don't like. He knows how hard I work to be good and kind. Listen, I'll repeat the verse for you. *"I will not take away his name from the book of life. I will say that he belongs to me before my Father and before his angels"* (Revelation 3:5).

I'm glad I'm in the book of life. When Jesus reads about me, I want that book to say I'm doing the best I can.

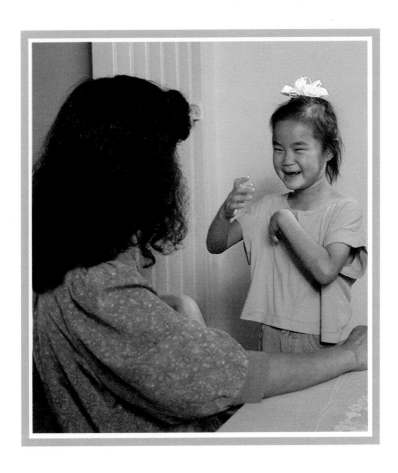

God Makes Me Happy

ome people are always sad. Some people are always mad. Not me. My mother says I'm the happiest person she's ever seen.

I laugh about stuff most of my friends get angry about. Like last week on the playground, I tripped and fell flat on my face. It didn't hurt, but I'm sure it must have looked funny. I laughed and laughed.

Yesterday, I spilled milk down my dress. My mother asked me if I was taking a milk bath. I laughed some more.

Of course, I don't laugh when someone else falls down or spills milk all over themselves. Only when I do it.

My mother showed me a verse in the Bible. She said it reminds her of me. *"Happy are the people whose God is the Lord" (Psalm 144:15).*

She's right. God loves me and will someday take us to heaven. Now that will make everybody happy!

God Will Fill My Life With Love

hen I play on a hot summer day, I get thirsty. I mean really thirsty. My mouth is dry. My tongue feels sticky. All I can think about is getting something to drink.

I run to the garden hose and enjoy some cool, refreshing water. It tastes great!

I drink and drink until I'm full. Then I can go back and play some more.

A few days ago, at church, I learned a new Bible verse. It says, *"Blessed are those who hunger and thirst for righteousness, for they will be filled" (Matthew 5:6, NIV)*. I asked my teacher what that verse meant. He said when a person wants Jesus to help him learn to be happy or teach him how to fight against Satan, Jesus will do it.

Now, when I get a drink from the garden hose, I think about that Bible text. I can fill my mouth with cool water, but Jesus wants to fill my life with love.

I Can Bring Joy to Angels

ave you ever been joyful? I sure have. When my daddy came home from a long trip, when my brother gave me a kitten for my birthday, and when my grandma came to visit me, I was very joyful. I jumped into the air and shouted, "Yeah!"

Maybe you've done that too. It feels great!

My daddy read me a text from the Bible that surprised me. It said, *"There is joy before the angels of God when 1 sinner changes his heart" (Luke 15:10)*. I don't know if the angels jump into the air like I do, but they might.

When I ask God to forgive me after I've done something wrong, I bring joy to heaven. God the Father smiles. Jesus, His Son, smiles. And the angels do whatever angels do when they're joyful.

Would you like to bring joy to heaven? Stop doing unkind things and start loving other people. Maybe you can make an angel jump for joy!

My friend Elizabeth isn't feeling well. The doctor told her she'll have to stay in bed for a long time.

"But you can take her some flowers," my mom said with a smile. "I think she and Jesus would like a visit from you."

"Jesus?" I asked. "I'm not visiting Jesus. Just Elizabeth."

Mom invited me to sit down beside her as she opened her Bible. "Well, maybe you'd better listen to this verse," she said. "'*[Jesus] will answer, "I tell you the truth. Anything you did for any of my people here, you also did for me"*' (*Matthew 25:40*). So you see, if you're kind to

I Can Do God's Work

someone, you're being kind to Jesus too."

I jumped up and ran to the door. "I'm going to pick some flowers for Elizabeth *and* Jesus," I shouted as I headed for the garden. "And I'll pick the prettiest ones. I want to make them both happy!"

God Will Help Me Live a Long Time

y stepmother is my best friend. She listens when I have a problem, helps me clean my room, and takes care of me when I'm sick.

I heard a Bible text that I didn't understand. Here's what it says. *"Honor your father and your mother. Then you will live a long time in the land" (Exodus 20:12).*

"What does *honor* mean?" I asked my stepmother.

"That means showing respect or thinking someone is important," she said.

"If I do that, I'll live a long time?" I asked.

My stepmother nodded. "When children honor those who take care of them, Jesus has promised a beautiful home in heaven, where we all can live forever. That's a very long time!"

I gave her a big hug. "Then I'm going to honor you every day," I said. "I want to live with you forever in heaven."

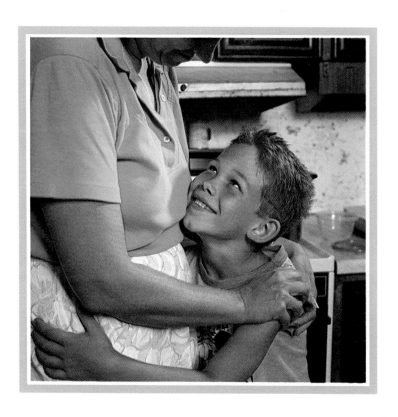

God Likes It When I Sing

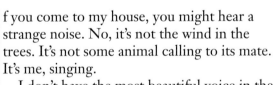

f you come to my house, you might hear a strange noise. No, it's not the wind in the trees. It's not some animal calling to its mate. It's me, singing.

I don't have the most beautiful voice in the world, but that's OK. God loves to hear me sing anyway.

I began doing this about a year ago when I learned a new Bible verse. Listen. I'll repeat it for you. *"The Lord is my strength and shield. I trust him, and he helps me. I am very happy. And I praise him with my song"* (Psalm 28:7).

I even made up my own songbook. It has all my favorite melodies in it. Dad says he thinks

God hears me best when I sit out in the back-
yard. Fine with me. Then I can have the birds
join in and the bees hum along. We make a
wonderful choir. What's your favorite song?
We can sing a duet!

ne winter day, I looked out the window and saw something that made me sad. There on a limb sat a little bird. He looked cold.

"Hey, Dad," I called. "There's a bird out in the snow. Maybe we should catch him and bring him inside, where it's warm."

Dad shook his head. "He'll be OK. You see, the same God who made the bird made the snow too. Birds don't mind the snow as long as they can get something to eat."

"God makes it snow?" I gasped.

God Brings the Snow

"Sure," Dad said with a smile. "I'll show you a verse that tells us so." He opened our big family Bible and read out loud, "'God says to the snow, "Fall on the earth." And he says to the rain shower, "Be a heavy rain"'" (Job 37:6). So you see, God brings both snow and rain to help the farmers and fill the wells so we can have water to drink."

I looked out at the little bird. "I'm glad Jesus cares for animals and people," I said. "He must love us very much."

I Am God's Child

orses are my favorite animals in the whole world. I love to watch them run across the meadow or play along the streams on our farm.

My dad says that people can learn a lot from horses. These animals work hard, obey their rider, and care for each other. Mommy horses watch over their little ones very tenderly. Daddy horses always protect their families. It's wonderful to see.

I'm learning a text in the Bible. Here, I'll read it to you. *"We should love each other, because love comes from God. The person who loves has become God's child and knows God"* (1 John 4:7).

My dad says that the Creator put love in all His creatures. Even horses know how to show it. We should too. He says when we care for others and protect them, we become children of God. Imagine! We can have two daddies—our regular daddy and a heavenly daddy. Isn't that a neat family?

I Don't Have to Be Afraid

 don't like wars. Sometimes the television announcer talks about a battle in one country or an army fighting in another country. It makes me afraid.

That's why God gave me a beautiful promise. It says, *"All your children will be taught by the Lord. And they will have much peace"* (Isaiah 54:13).

When there's peace, there are no wars, no fighting, no guns or bombs.

So, whenever I hear about war and feel afraid, I run to my mom or teacher and say, "Tell me what Jesus wants me to know." They smile and teach me how to be loving and for-

giving. And they tell me how much God loves me.

Then I'm not afraid anymore. I have peace in my heart.

 esterday, my friend Jared and I had a fight. It was his fault. Honest. Then he called me a sissy and went home. I was sad. Jared and I have been friends since we were little kids.

This morning, he called me on the telephone. He said, "I'm sorry for what I did yesterday. And I'm sorry I called you a sissy. Will you forgive me?"

That's when a Bible text I learned in church school popped into my mind. It says, *"Forgive other people, and you will be forgiven" (Luke 6:37)*. My teacher said God wants us to always forgive those who do bad things to us so He can forgive us when we do bad things to Him.

God Wants Me to Forgive Others

Well, I knew that included me, because I sometimes do stuff I shouldn't. Nobody's perfect.

"Sure, Jared," I said happily, "I forgive you. Would you like to come over and play Bible story? I'll be Esther, and you can be the king."

Jared said Yes, and soon we were having fun together. Forgiveness makes everyone, including God, feel a lot better.